Eliminate Goal-Setting?

Leadership Challenges for Servant Leaders

John J. Sullivan

Other books by John J. Sullivan

Servant First! Leadership for the New Millennium, Xulon Press, 2004

Seven Virtues, The Adventures of John Mouse, Xulon Press, 2010

Books in the series, Leadership Challenges for Servant Leaders:

My Betrayer is at Hand, CreateSpace, 2012

Details, Details, Details, CreateSpace, 2012

Truth Telling, CreateSpace, 2012

Severing the Ties That Bind, CreateSpace, 2012

Good News -- Bad News, CreateSpace, 2012

Eliminate Goal-Setting?, 2012

Dedicated to leaders and
followers who set stretch goals--
and achieve them

Preface

This is the sixth monograph in a series which addresses the most common leadership challenges in organizations today. Although the challenges are similar across organizations, the leadership styles which confront them are varied.

Leadership is leadership, whether one leads a small fellowship group or a large corporation, a squad or a corps, a team or an institution. What changes are the language (terms, acronyms) and the rules of engagement (how you interact with followers).

Interestingly, the more senior one becomes the more important are interpersonal relationships. This is counterintuitive at first glance but consider that as one leads larger and more complex organizations one becomes less and less an expert in what the organization does. The further one gets from "the product" the less one knows the product. Senior leaders become increasingly dependent upon followers who have the product expertise they lack; therefore the ability to build and maintain strong interpersonal relationships with core individuals within organizations is key to upper mobility and senior leader success.

This series is aimed at servant leaders or what Jim Collins calls Level 5 leaders[1]. This leadership model is best exemplified by the leadership style of Jesus of Nazareth who said He came to serve and not to be served. Leaders in industry, government, not-for-profit organizations and churches are discovering that

---

[1] Collins, Jim, *Good to Great: Why Some Companies Make the Leap . . . and Others Don't*, HarperCollins, 2001

the servant leader model is highly effective across organizational types.

This upside-down leadership style puts the needs of followers above those of the leader; promotes teamwork, individual dignity and worth; and results in a synergy of purpose unachievable with the old leadership models. Its application in today's organizations creates an environment in which people freely choose to create, innovate, and strive for excellence.

Enjoy this monograph on goal-setting and look for more books in this series *Leadership Challenges for Servant Leaders*.

Contents

Introduction

W. Edwards Deming's 11th Point for Management reads, "Eliminate management by objective. Eliminate management by numbers, numerical goals. Substitute leadership" (Deming, 1982). Was Deming really repudiating one of Peter Drucker's most respected tools for leaders, Management by Objectives? Does this mean that goal-setting is an inappropriate leadership tool? If you don't set goals how will you measure performance?

This is a widely misunderstood teaching point. Deming expounded his 11th Point by saying that, "internal goals set in the management of a company, without a method, are burlesque" (Deming, 1982, 75). He was arguing that objectives or goals cannot be set by leaders arbitrarily and that they must first have a detailed and complete understanding of the "system" in which they are working. If that system (the process that results in the good or service of the organization) is stable (variation is within normal limits) then there is no use to specify a goal. You will get whatever the system will deliver.! To emphasize his point, he reiterates, that "To manage, one must lead. To lead, one must understand the work that he and his people are responsible for" (Deming, 1982, 76).

I don't believe that Deming meant the elimination of goal-setting as a leadership tool. What he was opposed to was the misuse and abuse of goal-setting by leaders who had little or no knowledge of the processes under study. He opposed having leaders impose unrealistic goals upon employees which often caused them to behave in unethical and even illegal ways to meet those goals.

Drucker recognized the limitations of MBO when he said, "It's just another tool. It is not the great cure for management inefficiency" (Drucker, 1982). He emphasized that managers should focus on the result, not the activity. Objectives are the basis for work and assignments but measurements for the key areas of an organization are difficult to define (Drucker, 2001). Leaders must learn to delegate tasks by assigning responsibility without assigning a detailed plan for implementation. That should be the prerogative of the one being delegated. MBO is about setting objectives and then breaking those down into more specific goals or key results.

> Drucker emphasized that managers should focus on the result, not the activity

1

MBO Principles

The major principle behind MBO is to ensure that everyone within the organization has a clear understanding of the aims (objectives/goals) of the organization as well as their own roles and responsibilities in achieving those aims. According to Andy Grove, former CEO of Intel Corporation, "The one thing an MBO system should provide is focus" (Koteinikov, 2008). For MBO to be effective, individual managers must understand the specific objectives of their job and how those objectives fit in with the overall company objective set by senior leadership. "A manager's job should be based on a task to be performed in order to attain the company's objectives...the manager should be directed and controlled by the objectives of performance rather than by his boss" (Drucker, 1993).

Well then, what is the servant-first leader to do? Can she use goal-setting as a tool for performance measurement? The answer is emphatically YES! But it must be done the RIGHT way. Leaders must first realize that their people generally have the most knowledge about the processes in which they work. Leaders, even process experts, quickly lose that expertise once they are elevated to a supervisory position.

So the first step is to recognize that the person being evaluated has more knowledge about their process than the leader. They also know what is possible and what additional tools they may need to improve efficiency or expand effectiveness. Therefore the leader should first ask the employee to prepare a set of goals that promote specific objectives of their sub-organization (division, branch, office) which are, in turn, linked to the objectives of the super-organization (company, plant, church). Jack Stack, president and CEO of Springfield Remanufacturing Corporation, works with his senior leaders to ensure that "...these people know exactly what responsibilities and accountabilities they have for the coming year. I want the accountabilities to be very specific, at least 80% of them defined by financial ratios relating to things over which the person has total control. The final plan must not be just my plan" (Stack, 1997).

> Leaders must first realize that their people generally have the most knowledge about the processes in which they work.

2

SMART Goals

Goals must always support and promote the overall organizational goals and objectives. Their scope will be determined by the level of responsibility of the goal drafter. These are then reviewed with the leader until agreement is reached on a set of goals for the year (or quarter, month, etc.) These goals must be SMART:

- Specific

- Measurable

- Achievable

- Results-oriented, and

- Time-determined

Specific goals are goals that can be measured. "Improve customer satisfaction," is not a measurable goal. However, "reduce the number of customer complaint calls by 15% over the next 90 days," is. Your people know what is achievable and what is not based on the resources (tools, time, technology, expertise, funds, etc.) that you as the leader have provided for them. Goals should cause people to "stretch" yet not be unrealistic and therefore demotivating. Goals should point to specific results and a time for completion. How will you know whether or not you have achieved your goal if you have not determined when the goal is to be achieved?

Let's look at some examples of well-written goals and test each one to see if they are SMART.

Goal: to increase current sales of our entire product line to Wal-Mart Stores by 15% over the next six months

Is the goal SPECIFIC? Yes, it calls for a 15% increase across the board of our product line to Wal-Mart Stores.

Is the goal MEASUREABLE? Yes, the goal is stated as 15% increase from current sales.

Is the goal ACHIEVABLE? Yes, we believe that our goal is reasonable yet will require us to "stretch." This test is based upon the best judgment of the people "in the field" and closest to the customer. But it also may include demographic or other economic studies that project an opportunity for increased sales.

Is the goal RESULTS-ORIENTED? In other words, are we looking for a *specific* result? Again, the answer is yes, the goal is very specific and calls for a *specified* increase in *current year* sales across the *entire product line* with a *specific* customer (Wal-Mart Stores).

Finally, is the goal TIME-DETERMINED? Yes, we state the goal as being achieved over the *next six months*.

Goal: increase Sunday school attendance of college and young professionals by 25% over last year's average attendance

Before we begin to dissect this goal, we need to mindful of Tuckman's (1978) caution to make clear operational definitions.   We should first define the specific age group we are targeting.   What ages are included   in   the   group   of   "college   and   young professionals?" Do we only count the men and women between   the   ages   of   18   and   29   who   attend   the "college   and   young   professionals"   Sunday   school class? Or do we count anyone of that age group who attends any Sunday school class?   What occupations will we include in the "young professionals?"   What if someone is of the correct age but not in college or has a "blue collar" job?   Will that person count?   What constitutes   "attendance?"   Does   someone   need   to attend over 50% of the classes offered? How will we determine "average attendance?"   Again, we need to answer these questions ahead of time so that that there is no confusion or disagreement.   Just be clear about how you will define your target market.

Eliminate Goal-Setting?

3

The Leader's Attitude

Leaders who treat their employees with dignity and respect and jointly enter into goal-setting as a way to measure performance, enhance productivity and focus effort, will be surprised with the high standards that people will set for themselves.

The key to successful goal-setting is highly dependent upon the attitude with which the leader approaches the process. A servant-first leader will acknowledge the expertise, dignity and maturity of his employees and treat them accordingly. Your people will surprise you with goals that truly do lead to higher productivity.

Leaders who treat their employees with dignity and respect will be surprised with the high standards that people will set for themselves

Eliminate Goal-Setting?

References

Deming, W., (1982), *Out of the Crisis*, Cambridge: MIT

Drucker, P., (1982), *The Practice of Management*, New York: HarperCollins

Drucker, P., (1993), *Management: Tasks, Responsibilities, Practices*, New York: HarperCollins

Drucker, P., (2001), *The Essential Drucker*, New York: HarperCollins

Koteinikov, V. (2008), "Management by Objectives (MBO)," 1000ventures.com, http:www.1000ventures.com/business_guide/mgmt_mbo_main.html (7/18/2008)

Stack, J., (1997), The Curse of the Annual Performance Review, *Inc. Magazine*, March 1997

Tuckman, B., (1978). *Conducting Educational Research*. New York: Harcourt, Brace, Jovanovich

Eliminate Goal-Setting?

John J. Sullivan

About the Author

John J. Sullivan is the director of ServantLeader Ministries whose mission is to educate, encourage and equip leaders in all walks of life who desire to serve rather than be served.

He has had a wide variety of career experiences. He has served as a Marine Corps fighter pilot, a squadron and air station commander, senior staff officer, consultant, quality examiner, athletics director, professor, and conference commissioner. He is widely acclaimed as an authority on servant leadership as an author, a teacher and a practitioner.

A highly decorated Vietnam veteran, prior to entering academia he served for 28 years in the U.S. Marine Corps as a helicopter gunship pilot, fighter pilot, squadron commander, senior staff officer, base commander, and professor, retiring as a colonel. As a senior staff officer in the Pentagon, he was Program Coordinator for what was then the Department of the Navy's largest development and acquisition program, the F/A-18 Hornet aircraft. While he was the Commanding Officer, Marine Corps Air Station Beaufort, SC, the base was selected in worldwide competition as the best installation in the Marine Corps and received the prestigious Commander-in-Chief's Award for Installation Excellence.

He was the Course Director of Policy Making and Implementation within the National Security Decision Making Department and professor of management at the Naval War College, Newport, RI. He taught in the graduate program primarily in leadership education.

An American Society for Quality Certified Quality Manager, he was a founder of the Rhode Island Area Coalition for Excellence (RACE), helped design its State quality award, and was its first lead examiner.

Following his military career, Sullivan served for nine years as an associate professor of business at Montreat College, Montreat, NC. His teaching focus was in the disciplines of leadership and management.

He is a graduate of the University of Southern California, Webster University and the Naval War College.

Visit http://www.servantleaderministries.org for more information on servant leadership or the author.

www.ingramcontent.com/pod-product-compliance
Lightning Source LLC
Chambersburg PA
CBHW071604170526
45166CB00004B/1798